Bloody News From My Friend

Bloody News From My Friend

Poems by Siamanto

Translated by Peter Balakian
and Nevart Yaghlian

Wayne State University Press
Detroit

Grateful acknowledgment is made to the A.G.B.U. Alex Manoogian Cultural Fund for financial assistance in the publication of this volume.

LIBRARY OF CONGRESS CATALOGING-IN-PUBLICATION DATA

Siamantʻō, 1878-1915
 [Karmir lurer barekamēs. English]
 Bloody new from my friend / poems by Siamanto ; translated by
Peter Balakian and Nevart Yaghlian.
      p. cm.
 Includes bibliographical references (p.   ).
 ISBN 0-8143-2640-2640-4 (pbk. : alk. paper)
 I. Balakian, Peter, 1951-   II. Yaghlian, Nevart.   III. Title.
PK8548.S519K3713 1996
891´.99215–dc20   96-3047

Designer: Mary Krzewinski

Cover Art: The Genocide (1915–1917). *Historical Atlas of Armenia* (New York: Armenian National Education Committee, 1987).

Contents

Acknowledgments 7

Introduction by Peter Balakian 11

Grief 37

The Dance 41

The Bath 45

The Dagger 47

The Atonement 51

The Cross 53

The Son 57

Their Song 59

The Blind 63

The Mulberry Tree 67

Strangled 71

A Victory 75

Select Bibliography 79

Acknowledgments

I am grateful to my late great aunt Vergine Exerjian and to my late aunt Nona Balakian, who first introduced me to some of the poems in *Bloody News From My Friend*. Many thanks to Aram Arkun at the Krikor Zorhab Information Center at the Diocese of the Armenian Church for his scholarly aid and knowledge, and to my wife, Helen Kebabian, for her editorial help. Once again, a stay at Yaddo was instrumental in my completing the work on these poems and the introductory essay. The Colgate University Research Council gave generous support along the way. I am grateful to both.

—P.B.

I would like to thank Nubar Kupelian of the Armenian Department of the Diocese of the Armenian Church, and Gia Ayvazian, Librarian, Near Eastern Languages and Literature at UCLA for supplying a bibliography of literary criticism about Siamanto. I am also grateful to Arpine Khatchadourian, who evaluated the first draft of my literal translation and gave me helpful suggestions.

·—N.Y.

Grateful acknowledgment is made to the publications where some of these poems first appeared:
"Grief" and "The Dance" in *Against Forgetting: Twentieth Century Poetry of Witness*, ed. Carolyn Forché (W.W. Norton & Co., 1993).
"The Dagger" and "The Blind" in *Ararat*.
"The Cross" and "Strangled" in *Raft: A Journal of Armenian Poetry and Criticism*.

The first time it was reported that our friends were being butchered there was a cry of horror. Then a hundred were butchered. When a thousand were butchered and there was no end to the butchery, a blanket of silence spread.

—Bertolt Brecht

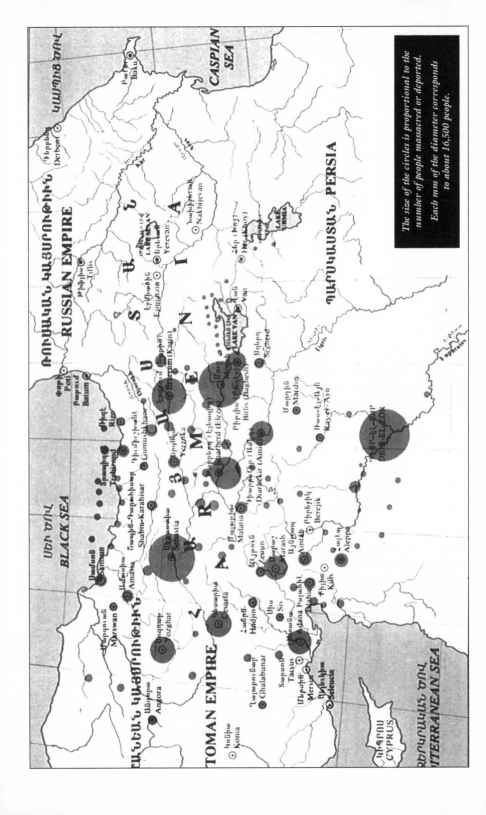

The size of the circles is proportional to the number of people massacred or deported. Each mm of the diameter corresponds to about 16,500 people.

Introduction

by Peter Balakian

My grandfather died more than a decade before I was born. But when conversation turned to him, there was sometimes mention of a book of poems with which he had something to do. In Armenia it was a famous book, written by his friend, Adom Yarjanian, whose pen name was Siamanto. Siamanto and my grandfather, Diran Balakian, were born in 1878 in Akn and Tokat, respectively, cities situated in the western part of Armenia Minor in central Anatolia, then ruled by the Ottoman Turkish government. As cosmopolitan Armenians, they went to Europe to complete their educations—my grandfather to medical school in Leipzig, and Siamanto to Paris, where he studied literature and philosophy.

After graduating from medical school in 1905, my grandfather returned to Constantinople to practice medicine. In 1909 he went with a group of Armenian physicians, responding to a crisis in the Adana region (historically known as Cilicia or Lesser Armenia) of south central Turkey. In Adana, in 1909 the Armenians were being massacred by the forces of the recently deposed Sultan and other counter-revolutionary groups. As in the Sultan's earlier massacres of 1895-96, Armenians were being scapegoated, and this time they were targeted because the purportedly liberal reforms the Young Turks were going to make would make Armenians equal citizens in the Ottoman Empire. Especially during the last two

Opposite: Map illustrating the Armenian Genocide (1915–1917). *Historical Atlas of Armenia* (New York: Armenian National Education Committee, 1987).

weeks of April, defenseless Armenians were butchered and burned alive by the thousands per day in what has been called "one of the most gruesome and savage bloodbaths ever recorded in human history."[1] Because hospitals, churches, and schools were the favorite targets, thousands of children and women were murdered en masse. Before the month was over, The Young Turks' army had also joined in, and so Armenians were being killed by the embittered reactionaries as well as the so-called liberals.

In 1915, the Young Turk government, led by Pashas Talaat, Enver, and Djemal, commenced their final solution for Armenia by implementing a systematic, premeditated genocide against the Armenian people, who were an unarmed, defenseless minority. A telegram of September 16, 1915 from Pasha Talaat to the government of Aleppo (then part of the Ottoman Empire) reads: "It was first communicated to you that by order of the Jemiet, 'The Ittihad Committee' had decided to destroy all the Armenians living in Turkey. Those who oppose this order and decision cannot remain on the official staff of the Empire. An end must be put to their existence however criminal the measures taken may be, and no regard must be paid to either age or sex or to conscientious scruples."[2]

The genocide perpetrated by the Turkish government against the Armenians was the most dramatic human rights issue of the first part of the twentieth century and was covered regularly under bold headlines in the *New York Times*. It remains a landmark in modern history because it is the first example of mass political killing implemented with the techniques and apparatus of the modern nation state, and it would serve, not surprisingly, as a paradigm for Hitler's final solution for the Jews of Europe. Only twenty-two years later, on August 22, 1939, Hitler remarked to his military advisors, "Who, after all, speaks today of the annihilation of the Armenians?"[3] The parallels between the Armenian Genocide and the Jewish Holocaust are significant. Both peoples were marginalized for their religious and cultural differences; first they were subject to harsh social discrimination, and finally they were demonized and massacred by fanatical nationalist and racist ideologies. By the end of 1918 the genocide had claimed well over a million Armenian lives, and the Turks had expunged all Armenian life everywhere in Turkey, except Constantinople and Smyrna—large international cities—thus wiping out a 3,000-year-old civilization which was situated on its homeland in central and eastern Anatolia.

The Adana massacres were both a prologue to the 1915 genocide, and a continuation of Abdul Hamid II's massacres of 1895–96, which claimed more than 200,000 Armenian lives. Although Turks would continue to massacre Armenians in Transcaucasia in the years following World War I, this period from 1895 through 1918 represents the major arc of the Turkish extermination policy against Armenians.

As the Ottoman Turkish Empire collapsed during the last decades of the nineteenth century and the first of the twentieth century, first losing the Balkan countries it had ruled for centuries, and then falling into deep debt accompanied by political corruption, its political leaders—Sultan Abdul Hamid II (1878–1908) and then the Young Turk government (1908–1918)—were using Armenians as scapegoats. By 1908 the Young Turk government was promoting a fanatical, racist nationalism known as pan-Turkism. The central tenet of this ideology was racial purity for Turkey; this ideology demonized all non-Turkic peoples, especially the Christian minorities—Armenians, Greeks, and Assyrians. For centuries, Christians in Turkey had been ostracized as "infidels," but the new pan-Turkism coalesced and accelerated this deep-seated bigotry.

As "infidels," Armenians for centuries had been relegated to outsider status. They were subject to an unjustly heavy tax burden and were deprived of legal rights in the Turkish courts. They were banned from occupations in the Turkish government, military, and civil service, and consequently were drawn to professional and commercial vocations, where they became successful and relatively wealthy. Their long-standing educational and intellectual traditions, and their ties to European culture and progressive thought, further widened the gulf between Armenians and Turks; a wealthy and educated Armenian Christian minority was a constant source of social resentment for the Turks. As this new, intensified climate of racism made conditions worse for Armenians, they formed political parties in order to seek civil rights and social reform. In this climate, the Sultan and the Young Turks found it easy to use the disproportionate relationship of wealth and education between the Armenian minority and the Turkish majority and the new Armenian reform movements as further pretexts for promoting race hatred. The Young Turks, as the Nazis later would, implemented their final solution behind the screen of a world war, when the world was enveloped in chaos, and it seemed possible to engage in mass killing in secrecy.

* * *

Diran Balakian worked in Adana in 1909, a physician aiding the victims of the massacres. He was an eyewitness to atrocities as only a physician could be, and saw daily the acts of torture performed by the Turkish gendarmes and civilians.

He was, as Camus described Dr. Rieux, his protagonist in *The Plague*, "well placed for giving a true account of all he saw and heard. . . . so that some memorial of the injustice done to them might endure."[4] He was unmarried (not marrying my grandmother until 1913) and he wrote letters home regularly to his family living in Constantinople. The letters, which have not survived, were filled with stark details and stories about the Adana atrocities. When Siamanto learned about my grandfather's letters, he dropped by the Balakian house to read them. Not only did he read the letters from Adana, but he used them as his source for this book of poems.

When my father wrote up his father's entry for the *National Cyclopedia of American Biography*, he wrote: "During 1909 he served with a group of Armenian doctors in Adana, Turkey, aiding stricken refugees of the Turkish massacres of those years. During that time he wrote a series of letters to his friend, the poet Siamanto, describing the conditions in Adana and the plight of the refugees, and these were published by the poet in 1911 under the name *Sanguinous* [my father's translation] *News From My Friend,* in both Armenian and English." My father's statement about his father's epistolary activities as an eyewitnessing doctor in the fields of death contains inaccuracies, but it is not without its larger significance. Siamanto didn't publish my grandfather's letters verbatim, and my grandfather didn't write verse. In writing the entry in the fashion that he did, my father was acknowledging how profoundly a joint venture this book of poems was: a physician and a poet collaborating to tell some truths.

Siamanto was executed on April 24, 1915 by the Turkish government. Like poets who live in dark times, as Brecht put it, Siamanto was the victim of a totalitarian government that perceived artists as dangerous and seditious. He was a poet whose identity and art were deeply bound up in his people and their political crisis. In this sense, he is a poet whose cultural situation bears resemblance to those of Yeats, Neruda, or Whitman during the Civil War. He meant what they meant, or have come to mean, to their cultures. He was a poet whose romance with his language and moral conviction about his people's plight were inseparable. Like Whitman, he believed that "a bard is to be commensurate with a people." And Siamanto was a poet of bardic affinities. He was a public poet who declaimed his poems before audiences and crowds, continuing an Armenian bardic tradition that had medieval roots and is probably best exemplified and known in the life and poetry of the eighteenth-century poet Sayat Nova.

It is important for the reader unfamiliar with Armenian letters to understand that Siamanto was part of an extraordinary moment in Armenian intellectual history. In the second half of the nineteenth century both Eastern Armenia (Transcaucasian Armenia in the Russian Empire) and Western Armenia (Anatolian Armenia in the Ottoman Turkish Empire) were enjoying a cultural renaissance. From the second half of the eighteenth century on, both Eastern and Western Armenia had absorbed a good deal of intellectual culture from Europe and Russia. The Enlightenment and Romanticism had done much to modernize Armenian writers and thinkers. Voltaire, Racine, and Hugo alone brought the message of civil liberty and human equality to Armenian writers who were eager to seize the tools of the Enlightenment to help them address the deplorable political condition of Armenians in the Ottoman Empire.

Although the impact of French culture on Armenia in the nineteenth century seems to have been preeminent, Byron and Shelley, Swift, Milton, and Shakespeare also contributed their share to Armenia's intellectual revival, as did the Italian Risorgimento, by way of the Armenian monastery on the island of San Lazaro in Venice. There, Mekhitarist monks—who had taken in Byron in 1816 for a year of studying classical Armenian—were a bridge between Armenia and Italy since 1717. Manzoni and Leopardi were translated frequently by Armenians from the middle of the nineteenth century on. To Armenians the radical events of 1848 in France, along with Lamartine, Hugo, and Proudhon, became signposts of progress and the ideals of human freedom.

While nineteenth-century European influences helped shape Siamanto, so did a revival of interest in classical and medieval Armenian art and culture. Like many European cultures, Armenia in the late nineteenth century was involved in its own Romantic movement, and writers and artists were rediscovering pre-Christian and early Christian poetry such as the epic of David of Sassoun and the spiritual lamentations of the monk Gregory of Nareg. The ballad tradition of Sayat Nova and Armenian folk music—which the priest and composer Gomidas was collecting, arranging, and using in his own compositions—were revitalized. New scholarly and artistic interests in thirteenth and fourteenth century manuscript painting, early Christian architecture, and other decorative arts like stone carving and rug weaving, provided an influx for sensibility and imagination.

In this milieu, Siamanto came to a more comprehensive and sophisticated understanding of Armenian culture than poets of an earlier generation might have. By the early part of the twentieth century Armenian writers had begun producing the dynamic forms that occur when native traditions and political predicaments collide with the ideas and techniques of other cultures, in this case French, Italian, German, and English. Armenian writers of this modern period became cosmopolitan in ways that they had not been for centuries.

The Mehian literary movement, for example—which was centered in Constantinople around Siamanto, Daniel Varoujan, Gostan Zarian, Krikor Zorhab, Shant, and others— was Armenian Modernism, and it mingled with Italian Futurism and German Expressionism. What is haunting to think about now is how this generation of vanguard Western Armenian writers was executed by the Turkish government (as were many Armenian intellectuals and statesmen in April of 1915) just as they were maturing and beginning to create an Armenian literature that was dynamic and new. Naturally, with the destruction of Western Armenia, Western Armenian literature was strangled, but its influence on successive generations of Armenian writers in Armenia, the Soviet Union, Europe, and the United States has been profound.

* * *

There is nothing like *Bloody News From My Friend* that I know of in the twentieth century. It is a book that was forged from certain salient late nineteenth-century literary modes, but somehow along the way turned into something startling and original. The *Bloody News* poems undermine our traditional ideas about genre. For, while they adhere to certain Victorian poetic conventions such as dramatic monologue and a dialogic epistolary voice, they are lyric poems in a different key. It is clear that the intrusion of genocidal violence in Siamanto's imagination gave rise to a poetic language that is raw and blunt. It is often a language that eschews metaphor and symbol for a starker presentation. Like the

British World War I poets, Siamanto found that the impact of political violence was subversive to the poetic gentility of much late nineteenth-century poetry in Europe and the United States. For him, "political intrusion"—the term is Terrence Des Pres'—became a radicalizing factor.[5]

In wrestling with "raw evil," as Siamanto puts it, the poems often deal with folkloric and ethnographic aspects of traditional Armenian culture. Because Armenians were uprooted from their traditional life by Turkish political violence, he was obsessed with Turkish capacity to demonize the other, in this case, Christian Armenians. Because what happened to Armenians happened also to the Greeks who were living in western Anatolia and the Pontus, especially in their ancient cities of Constantinople and Smyrna, and to the Christian Assyrians of eastern Anatolia, these poems speak for the experience of those peoples, too. Poems like "The Bath," "The Dagger," "The Atonement," "The Cross" are full of blood but are not sensationally indulgent. They are horrifying and grotesque but not romantic. They depict the ways Turkish people, ordinary citizens, treated Armenian men and women, whom they considered *giaours* or infidels. "Bloodthirsty" is a word that Siamanto uses again and again, and I suspect it was a word my grandfather used in his letters home.

Henry Morgenthau, the United States ambassador to Turkey between 1913 and 1916, in his famous Armenian Genocide memoir, *Ambassador Morgenthau's Story*, wrote:

> I have by no means told the most terrible details, for a complete narration of the sadistic orgies of which these Armenian men and women were the victims can never be printed in an American publication. Whatever crimes the

most perverted instincts of the human mind can devise, and whatever refinements of persecution and injustice the most debased imagination can conceive, became the daily misfortunes of this devoted people. I am confident that the whole history of the human race contains no such horrible episode as this. The great massacres and persecutions of the past seem almost insignificant when compared with the sufferings of the Armenian race.[6]

Those "sadistic orgies" are at the center of *Bloody News From My Friend*. "The Bath" and "The Cross," for example, raise moral and philosophical questions about the relationship between religion and power. Do Siamanto's poems about Turkish people torturing, murdering, and in some cases cannibalistically devouring Armenians lead us to conclude that religious systems are the means through which the state implements its world-view, to evoke Durkeim? Or, are we to draw connections and parallels between these Turkish acts of sadism and genocide and our contemporary experience of Islamic fundamentalist violence? I'm inclined to agree with Ambassador Morgenthau's conclusion that the men who implemented the genocide—Talaat, Enver, and their circle— were atheistic cynics, but that the peasants, the provincial bureaucrats, and gendarmes—that is, the ordinary citizens— often slew Armenians as a service to Allah, and were motivated by religious ideology. Siamanto's obsession with *the other* is bound up in his need to probe the psychic mechanisms of Turkish Islam and its mode of rationalizing wholesale murder.

It is extraordinary to see how in writing about genocide with such blunt realism, Siamanto wrote poems that are remarkably modern in their concreteness, their unromanticized view of the world, their daring risks with vernacular, their ways of using the epistolary episode and eyewitness-like reportage. Many of the qualities that Ezra Pound and the Modernists would extol in the ensuing decade, Siamanto had already discovered by virtue of his hybridized sensibility and his political predicament as an Armenian.

* * *

Indeed, if a poetry of witness is defined by its bearing a trace of the event, as Carolyn Forché has suggested,[7] or by simply representing, in the domain of its own particular imaginative realm, some dimension of the human brutality which defines the event, then Siamanto's poems surely bear witness. For he has come back from hell to tell us some truths about what humans are capable of doing to other humans. And in the communal nature of the epistolary idea of these poems, the poet makes it clear that this genocidal horror must be conveyed to the world for the very sake of morality. The voice at the opening of "The Cross" says, "I want to testify about what's happening to our orphaned race."

Poetry, no matter what its claim to truth, must always maintain its creative freedom, and so its symbolic strategies and transformations, ironic orchestrations and distancing are always significant. The point of view and framing techniques in most of these poems are crucial to Siamanto's way of maintaining truth, lyric integrity, and some distancing that creates its own conventions of irony. As the title suggests, the poet has received, from his friend, eyewitness accounts of what has happened to his Armenian countrymen and women in the hinterlands, in this case in the province of Adana in 1909.

Introduction

Because Diran Balakian, the physician, had sent letters home, which were read by his friend the poet, Siamanto, the poet's distance is an established part of the book's perspective. Many of the poems begin *in medias res* as the correspondent writes home, in order to dramatize how an event is being passed from a witness to a third party, while in other poems, like "The Dagger," or "The Cross," the voice of epistolary witness speaks openly: "I don't want this letter to scare you," or "Forgive me today my good friend of old dreams." In modes of rhetorical engagement, then, the poems convey the authority of one who is seeing through the eyes of others who have survived or perished—the displaced, the wandering, the uprooted.

Furthermore, the poems are framed by dramatic techniques: notably, dramatic monologue and dialogue. "The Dance" is told by a German woman, an eyewitness who has become involved in helping Armenian victims. As she nurses a dying woman, she watches from her window the torture, mutilation, and immolation of twenty Armenian women who are forced to dance—a method of killing women that became common during the Genocide. In "The Mulberry Tree," an Armenian woman, a deportee, tells the story of an old woman who has gone mad after seeing her grandson killed. In "Strangled," "A Victory," and "The Son," an omniscient voice tells tales of heroism and horror. "Strangled," for example, deals with a mother who is forced to suffocate her infant so that a group of Armenians hiding in a cellar won't be found by Turkish soldiers.

Not only do these dramatic voices provide Siamanto with distanced perspective, but his interest in *the other* allows him to engage his craft in order to investigate the sadism of Turkish culture. The poems ask: How can people engage in wanton cruelty? What motivates them? How do they demonize the ethnic other, in this case the Christian Armenian? One must remember that during this period the Young Turk government promoted a xenophobic racism called pan-Turkism, which glorified the Turkic people and called for the removal of all non-Turkic peoples, especially Armenian and Greek Christians, who were deemed *giaours* or infidels. The parallels with Hitler's Aryanism are striking.

* * *

As the poems observe the intimate details of torture and murder, we witness the Turkish obsession with killing Christians in the name of Allah. In "The Cross," a poem told by an omniscient witness, who says "I want to testify about what's happening to our orphaned race," a mother pleading for her son in a church is met by a Turkish mob and some gendarmes. "Don't worry," they tell her, "He's in the vestibule praying for you . . . he'll be free today." They strip her, soak her dress in his blood, and make her smell it. "Doesn't it smell familiar?" they taunt her. Then they paint a cross in blood on the chapel wall, and the poem closes:

> In the church that Turk pointed to the cross.
> "Kneel down and pray.
> We'll do it to you like you did it to Christ.
> Hey, mother, pray to your son.
> Have you no faith in the resurrection?"

The ritualized blood thirst in some of these poems is a kind of representation of genocidal psycho-pathology. In "The Atonement," a pious, wealthy Turkish man decides he must avenge the one sin of his life, "the black day when lusting over / an Armenian beauty / he shrugged his daily prayer." The only way to repent is for him to slaughter an Armenian boy and drink his blood. As the poem closes, he dies drinking the boy's blood from a gold cup.

Images of sexual violence—rape and torture—shape the landscapes of so many of these poems, that one is forced to note something about the deep-seated misogyny of patriarchal Turkish society. During the Genocide, Armenian men were the first to be rounded up, usually in the town square, and killed, so that the women and children would be left defenseless. If they weren't raped and killed, the women were often taken to Turkish or Kurdish homes where they were forced to convert to Islam and marry. Yet, even before the Genocide, Armenian women lived in constant fear of sexual assault. Armenian men, because of their infidel status, were often ill-equipped to protect them, and the quartering act, which allowed Turkish and Kurdish men—most often nomadic farmers—to live in Armenian houses during the winter months, often meant rape and abduction for the women of those houses.

In poems like "The Blind" and "The Dagger," the sadistic piety involved in sexual violence is shocking. In "The Blind," a blind old Turkish man, making his way through the "bloodthirsty mob"—the mob that is ubiquitous in these poems—expresses a popular Turkish attitude toward Armenians:

"I don't even know the visage of the infidel.
What monster, what reptile, what black snake does it
    resemble?
How badly I want to feel a dead body with my hands."

Fighting for Allah, the old man says, "My blindness shouldn't deprive me of my heaven. / Bring me a virgin whose body's tender as a dove." His son's friend then brings him a young Armenian woman who has refused to marry the Turkish boy and become a Muslim. "The naked girl writhed like an enraged wave," and as the blind man kills her with a dagger, his face is splattered with blood, and he cries out "My eyes are clear. I've seen the light."

In "The Dagger," sexual violence and sadism are inseparable from the Turkish envy of Armenian wealth. Notwithstanding their second-class citizenry, many Armenians were wealthier than their Turkish counterparts, and this fueled further resentment against them. In this epistolary poem the witness refers to Armenia's "hope for Brotherhood" going up in flames, as an Armenian family's wealth becomes the focus of hatred. As a Turkish man dresses the Armenian woman in her own jewels before killing her, he shouts, "Don't beg me sweetie, I hate tears . . . I love these brooches in your hair." Then, with the family's dagger—an image which evokes the Turkish paranoia about Armenians as seditious—he tries to force the woman to kill her son. "Feast your eyes one last time on your wealth, you infidel, / because I'm distributing all this stuff to my friends." Instead of killing her son, she kills herself, but then one of the mob takes the dead woman's hand with the dagger and stabs the son seven times. In ritualistic fashion, the son is killed on an ivory table in the family parlor—"Let's use your ivory table as an altar"—and once again, Siamanto depicts an image of crucifixion that is not melodrama but a realistic representation of the Turkish disdain for the culture of *the other*.

Other poems dramatize the relationship between religion and power in ways that disclose how deeply religious ideas and existing social structures were used to motivate

Turkish people to commit genocide. "The Bath," for example, is about a Turkish sorceress who prescribes for an infertile Turkish woman a bath in the blood of seven sixteen-year-old Armenian girls. After the girls are butchered, the poem closes with the simple detail of a ritual, as the "warm blood of the virgins / began to rise from her feet / up her legs to her womb."

Elaine Scarry, in *The Body In Pain*, her pioneering study of torture, war, and human expression, remarks, "what is remembered in the body is well remembered,"[8] a phrase that suggests so much of what is terrifying in these poems. For Siamanto confronts pain, bodily destruction, and torture as few modern poets have. Scarry's assertion that torture is "the undoing of civilization" underscores the ambition of Siamanto's lyric poems, and in some way "the body in pain" is an apt trope for the *Bloody News* poems. In studying Amnesty International records of torture victims of contemporary totalitarian regimes, Scarry also sheds light on the structure of Turkish torture in the earlier part of the century. Torture, she notes, is a totalizing infliction of bodily pain, such that the victim is rendered speechless and is subjugated, in the most complete sense, to the power of the regime. Survivor testimony and eyewitness accounts document fully the extent of Turkish torture during the Genocide. Eye-gouging, bastinadoing, fingernail plucking, dismemberment, slow methods of castration, were only some of the forms of torture inflicted by the Turkish special police. It's hardly coincidental that Siamanto was himself a victim of Turkish torture in 1915, in large part for writing these poems. But, as the grandmother in "The Mulberry Tree" testifies when she grieves over the loss of her domestic life, this kind of violence unmakes the world:

You should've seen my home, what a hearth of good
     things—
lambs, hens, a white cock.
Everything in my sheepfold burnt down.
In my granary I had a handful of wheat for autumn,
under my garret two bee-hives.
In one day the whole village was burned.
Every morning smoke puffed out my chimney.
What did the Turks want from me? Tell me. . .

Torture, Scarry notes, unmakes human consciousness,
cuts the self off from the world entirely, breaks and severs
the voice. The tortured are rendered in isolation, their bod-
ies solitary and exposed. In our literature, she notes, such
conditions are rarely given expression. Siamanto's poems
suggests at least one way to give voice to the tortured. The
voiceless are restored to human community for the eternal
moment that the poem creates. All these representative vic-
tims of torture and ultimately genocide are rendered in their
agony by the poet, who returns a voice to their wretched-
ness. If genocide, as the extrapolation of torture, is the
emblem of power the totalitarian government creates to wipe
out its victims, these poems can be seen as heroic resistance:
a refusal to let the victims go voiceless into the dust. In their
sense of gesture and primal agony, these poems convey
what Scarry calls "sounds anterior to language."[9] For the
wretched in the *Bloody News* poems are often rendered
speechless or seen in gestures suggesting the limits of lan-
guage. At the end of "The Mulberry Tree," the companion of
the narrator, having seen the grandmother go crazy, begins
to "cry like a child." In the closing line of "The Dance," the
German narrator implies a world beyond words, "How can I
dig out my eyes?" and "Strangled" concludes with the moth-

er who has strangled her infant begging for her own death, which embodies the end of speech.

The whole cycle of poems can be seen as a representation of the traumatized body. The image of the German woman at the end of "The Dance," who asks "how can I dig out my eyes?" suggests the complexity of witnessing. For the witnessing woman makes a paradoxical gesture that suggests that the horror is, in some way, beyond perception and comprehension. To witness the torture and immolation of the women compels her to wish for the erasure of her own gaze; but this gesture toward self-blinding is also one of empathy with the victims. What our witness tells us is that it is not possible to be a passive bystander. Thus, her response is an expression of self-mutilation that is at once empathic and outraged beyond the parameters of body-knowledge.

In one sense, the moral appeal of this cycle of poems derives its force from these ethical realities. It is significant and certainly not ironic that torture in Turkey in the 1980s was so "widespread and systematic," according to Amnesty International that in 1985 Amnesty International published a special book, *Turkey: Testimony On Torture*.[10] The Turkish government's repressive and brutal treatment of its Kurdish population today only dramatizes how the voices of Siamanto's Armenian victims echo outward into our century.

* * *

While many of the *Bloody News* poems rely on narrative conventions, a poem like "Grief" is a wonderful example of Siamanto's more lyric and bardic power. The poem's rhetoric conveys a Horatian sense of the poet's civic persona. Siamanto addresses a man and woman, who are Armenian cultural emblems: "unknown sister / or brother of fate," he calls them. "You, stranger, soulmate, / who leaves behind the road of joy, / listen to me." Given that the poet is speaking for his people's predicament in a time of crisis, the sense of collectivity underscores every innuendo of the poem. What is deeply personal and what is dramatically public merge. The sense of historical moment is important to the poem's fullest meaning. For the poem is directly about the sense of betrayal Armenians felt after the massacre at Adana in 1909. With the overthrow in 1908 of Abdul Hamid II, Turkey's last sultan, Armenians believed a new dawn of egalitarianism and civil reform had arrived, and that the Young Turk government would bring, as it had promised, some degree of Western democracy to Turkey. In 1908 the Armenian mood was optimistic. For the bloody purges of 1895–96, which had taken the lives of more than 200,000 Armenians, was—at that time—the nadir of Armenian history under Turkish rule.

What happened, of course, was a shock. As it turned out, the Young Turk regime's idea of nationalism was based on a fanatical racism. The idealism of Armenian civil rights reform was dashed within a year. "Foreign hands," Siamanto writes, "yanked out / the sublime rose of freedom /. . . Let its divine scent intoxicate everyone." The slaughter of innocents becomes the grieving tone of the cycle—"I know your innocent feet are still wet with blood"—and is an apt prologue to the genocidal period that was beginning. The figures in this poem are foreshadowing, for they are already exiled and wandering. At the closing of the journey, the protagonists return to their houses, but the "wicked Capital" is menacing, and the future is grim. Siamanto's gift for wry bitterness and surreal-like humor in the face of atrocity are nowhere better heard than in the middle of the fourth stanza:

walk down the roads without rage or hate
and exclaim: what a bright day,
what a sarcastic grave-digger. . .
what a mob, what dances, what joy
and what feasts everywhere. . . .
Our red shrouds are victory flags.
The bones of our pure brothers are flutes. . .
with them others are making strange music.

These surrealistic images become inventive twists of gallows humor and a brave and idealistic reply to evil. Siamanto isn't afraid to risk the broad moral rhetoric that comes with his Horatian stance, as he exclaims to the Armenian country folk, "if you are chased down by raw Evil, / don't forget that you are born / to bring forth the fruitful Good." Or, "The law of life stays the same. . . / human beings can't understand each other."

* * *

Working with my collaborator and friend, Nevart Yaghlian, who provided me with literal translations and her well-spring of literary and linguistic intelligence, I did my best to render these poems into an idiom that best corresponds with my sense of late-twentieth-century American poetry. I believe that a translator must bring a poet's language from one historical time into the language of the present. The differences between Henry Wadsworth Longfellow's 1867, John Ciardi's 1954, and Robert Pinsky's 1994 translations of Dante's *Inferno* remind us how profoundly translation changes and reinvigorates the original.

Because I felt that Siamanto's oratorical style does not have an effective equivalent in English, I did not try to reproduce all of the sound play that exists in the original

Armenian, and at times this has led me to edit and trim lines. Thus, I felt liberated to pursue a slightly freer line and to make contemporary some of the dialogue, which was contemporary in its own time and so should read with as much idiomatic, vernacular language as possible in our age. For in using vernacular speech, Siamanto was truly interested in capturing the criminal mentality of the Turkish people who engaged in genocide. Regardless of whatever changes I have made, I have remained faithful to the meaning, the spirit, the ideas, the reality of images, and the voice in these poems, and I have done my best to create the same sense of response in our audience as Siamanto did in his audience.

Bloody News From My Friend was first published in Constantinople in 1909, and a year later the book was published in an edition of Siamanto's *Complete Poems*, in Armenian, by the Hairenik Press of Boston, where Siamanto was living at the time. In 1985 The Donikian Press of Beiruit reissued *Bloody News From My Friend*. While a couple of the poems have appeared in various anthologies including *Anthology of Armenian Poetry* (Diana Der Hovanessian and Marzbed Margossian, Columbia University Press, 1978) and Balakian and Yaghlian's translations of "The Dance" and "Grief," in *Against Forgetting: Twentieth Century Poetry of Witness* (ed. Carolyn Forché, W.W. Norton & Co., 1993), this is the first time this book has appeared in English, and the first time most of these poems have been translated into English.

Looking back at *Bloody News From My Friend* from the end of the twentieth century, one can sense something postmodern about the disruptive strategies of these poems. It seems to me that *Bloody News From My Friend* makes more sense to us in the late twentieth century than it did when they were first published in Constantinople in 1909. In refusing to be ornamental, generic, or metaphysical, Siamanto insisted on seeing in a clear way the political horrors that have come to define our century; his vernacular freedom and his evocative ethnographies are similarly unique and groundbreaking. To read a simple line from "The Son" is to encounter a prophetic emblem, written in 1909, for a century marred by genocidal violence and war: "For miles, the cinders of farms, strewn corpses, / and in his living room his wife, naked and stabbed." Even before the British poets of World War I found themselves stuck in the trenches, Siamanto's encounter with evil disclosed how political violence can alter the poetic imagination.

Notes

1. Vahakan Dadrian, *The History of the Armenian Genocide* (Providence, R.I. and Oxford: Berghahn Books, 1996), p. 183.

2. Aram Andonian, intro. in Viscount Gladstone, *Memoirs of Niam Bey: Turkish Official Documentation Relating to the Deportations and Massacres of the Armenians* (London: Hodder & Stoughton, 1920), p. 64.

3. K. B. Bardakjian, *Hitler and the Armenian Genocide* (Cambridge, Mass: Zoryan Institute, 1985), p.1.

4. Albert Camus, *The Plague*, trans. Stuart Gilbert (New York: Random House, 1972), pp. 270, 287.

5. Terrence Des Pres, *Praises and Dispraises* (New York: Viking, 1988), p. 2.

6. Henry Morgenthau, *Ambassador Morgenthau's Story* (New York: Doubleday, Page & Co., 1919), pp. 321–22.

7. Carolyn Forché, ed., *Against Forgetting: Twentieth Century Poetry of Witness* (New York: W. W. Norton & Co., 1993), p. 31.

8. Elaine Scarry, *The Body In Pain* (New York: Oxford University Press, 1985), p. 110.

9. Ibid., p. 54.

10. Turkey: *Testimony on Torture* (London: Amnesty International Publications, 1985).

Bloody News From
My Friend

In this way we drink the still hot blood of our wounds.

—L. Deyerks

Grief

You, stranger, soul-mate,
who leaves behind the road of joy,
listen to me.
I know your innocent feet are still wet with blood.
Foreign hands have come and yanked out
the sublime rose of freedom,
which finally bloomed from the pains of your race.

Let its divine scent intoxicate everyone,
Let everyone—those far away, your neighbor, the
            ungrateful,
come and burn incense
before the goddess of Justice
that you carved from stone with your hammer.
Proud sowers, let others reap with your scythes
the wheat that ripens in the gold earth you ploughed.
Because if you are chased down by raw Evil,
don't forget that you are born
to bring forth the fruitful Good.

Walk down the avenues of merriment,
and don't let the happy ones see in your eyes

that image of corpse and ash.
Spare the passerby, whether a good man or a criminal.
Because Armenian pain
rises up in the eyes' visage.
As you walk through the crossroad of merriment,
don't let a speck of gladness or a tear
stain grief's majesty.
Because for the vanquished, tears are cowardly
and for the victors, the smile is frivolous, a wrinkle.

Armenian woman, with veils darkening you like death.
You, young man with native anguish
running down your face,
walk down the roads without rage or hate
and exclaim: what a bright day,
what a sarcastic grave-digger. . .
what a mob, what dances, what joy
and what feasts everywhere. . . .
Our red shrouds are victory flags.
The bones of our pure brothers are flutes. . .
with them others are making strange music.
But don't shudder, unknown sister
or brother of fate.
As you study the stars
take heart, go on.
The law of life stays the same. . .
human beings can't understand each other.

And this evening before sunset
all of you will go back to your houses,

whether they are mud or marble,
and calmly close the treacherous
shutters of your windows.
Shut them from the wicked Capital,
shut them to the face of humanity,
and to the face of your god. . . .
Even the lamp on your table
will be extinguished
by your soul's one clear whisper.

The Dance

In a field of cinders where Armenian life
was still dying,
a German woman, trying not to cry
told me the horror she witnessed:

"This thing I'm telling you about,
I saw with my own eyes.
Behind my window of hell
I clenched my teeth
and watched the town of Bardez turn
into a heap of ashes.
The corpses were piled high as trees,
and from the springs, from the streams and the road,
the blood was a stubborn murmur,
and still calls revenge in my ear.

Don't be afraid. I must tell you what I saw,
so people will understand
the crimes men do to men.
For two days, by the road to the graveyard. . . .

Let the hearts of the world understand.
It was Sunday morning,

the first useless Sunday dawning on the corpses.
From dawn to dusk I had been in my room
with a stabbed woman—
my tears wetting her death—
when I heard from afar
a dark crowd standing in a vineyard
lashing twenty brides
and singing filthy songs.

Leaving the half-dead girl on the straw mattress,
I went to the balcony of my window
and the crowd seemed to thicken like a clump of trees.
An animal of a man shouted, 'You must dance,
dance when our drum beats.'
With fury whips cracked
on the flesh of these women.
Hand in hand the brides began their circle dance.
Now, I envied my wounded neighbor
because with a calm snore she cursed
the universe and gave up her soul to the stars. . . .

'Dance,' they raved,
'dance till you die, infidel beauties.
With your flapping tits, dance!
Smile for us. You're abandoned now,
you're naked slaves,
so dance like a bunch of fuckin' sluts.
We're hot for your dead bodies.'
Twenty graceful brides collapsed.
'Get up,' the crowd screamed,
brandishing their swords.

Then someone brought a jug of kerosene.
Human justice, I spit in your face.
The brides were anointed.
'Dance,' they thundered—
'here's a fragrance you can't get in Arabia.'

With a torch, they set
the naked brides on fire.
And the charred bodies rolled
and tumbled to their deaths. . . .

I slammed my shutters,
sat down next to my dead girl
and asked: 'How can I dig out my eyes?'"

The Bath

Her body was white
as God's snow on the Taurus Mountains,
and her eyes burned with passion and fear,
because this black-haired Turkish beauty was barren,
her breasts dry.

Drunk with the need
for a wild man to save her,
this sullen girl didn't realize
that the great Order had its iron secret . . .
but in these days of ravage
a Turkish sorceress said:
"If you want your diamond-hard womb to bear fruit
I'll give you the ancient remedy,"
and her eyes flashed with lightning
as she chanted the folklore of cruelty.

Then they brought from our quiet village
seven sixteen-year-old Armenian virgins.
I can see your tragic fate is the same,
poor sisters of my inevitable death march.

Seven sixteen-year-olds shivering with fear
pushed through the marble doors of a bathhouse
where the rays of the sun rained on
a wooden tub adorned with white lilies.
Behind a curtain the sorceress
chanted as the Turkish woman
threw her gold veils to her maid-servants,
stripping peacefully.

The men in black
pulled out their daggers
and slit the throats of the virgins of our village.

Looking toward heaven, the petrified barren beauty
rose to her feet,
as the warm blood began to rise
up her legs to her womb.

The Dagger

I don't want this letter to scare you.
Your heart, like our bloody soil
and the olive branch of our hope for Brotherhood,
will burn again in the flame of all this.

"Listen, you rich Armenian,
I'm your master now.
Don't beg me for anything.
If I send you to hell, you'll go.

I've invited neighbors and friends
from nearby towns,
and they're eager to sit and watch.

Bring me this lady's jewelry box.
I'm going to make her glitter.
Hey friends, what a flood of jewels,
this could outshine the sun.

Come here, dear, let me dress your guilty wrists.
These ruby earrings glitter on your ears.
Gimme your hands, a garnet ring on each finger.
Already they look like your son's flowing blood.

Don't beg me, sweetie, I hate tears,
this necklace is hot rocks on your throat.

What's the crescent next to this?
I love these brooches in your hair, too. Diamonds?

Pick your own slippers. Gold or pearl?
And look at your son one last time.
You can even nurse him.
He came out of you, didn't he?

Step right up, friends and neighbors,
this toddler has eyes like his father,
and I used this same dagger to kill him this morning.
Did he bequeath you his vengeance?

Friends, for love of Mohammed, you tell me.
For whom had this lovely couple hidden this dagger?
For us?"

"Yeah, for us," screamed the friends in the hallway.

"Let's use your ivory table as an altar.
Feast your eyes one last time on your wealth, infidel,
because I'm distributing all this stuff to my friends.

Grip the dagger, and rip it over your son's chest.
Are you hoping? Which faith? Resurrection?
Hurry up, bitch, I hear the muezzin, we'll be late for
        prayer."

The woman swung her dagger heavenward,
then collapsed dead, her eyes open.
But some blood-thirsty punk took her dead hand
with the dagger in it, and stabbed her son seven times.

The Atonement

One morning an old man
looked into the pond of his vineyard,
and saw the one sin of his past well up.

He closed his eyes and saw
the black day when lusting over
an Armenian beauty
he shrugged his daily prayer.

Reliving those bloody days
he recalled the brightness of that fine girl,
when deceived by her marble flesh
he forgot about prayer.

Now as the delirium of lust died down,
and he heard his grave being dug,
his guilt deepened,
and he longed to atone.

The bell of righteousness rang
as he walked up the steps of his estate
and called his servant to the gold hallway,
where he sat like a sultan in his mother-of-pearl chair

on a silk rug with nightingales
singing their love to the false fragrant rose,
and his extended family, even his new grandchildren
knelt around him on those sprawling flowers.

Then two black men took a fair Armenian boy from
       Darson
to the cellar and with a scimitar slashed off his
       clothes.
His death shriek shook the house,
and a statuesque veiled servant came
to tell him that the deed was done.
"I'm not worthy of the dust on your feet,"
she said, "who shall offer you the cup of atonement?"

"There's no doubt," he said:
"The last child of that Armenian girl
who cost me my place in paradise."

So that grandchild brought him a silver tray
with a gold cup filled with blood.
"You unlucky ones, this cup is a symbol of your
       defeat,"
and he bit into the cup
and on the threshold of his paradise
he smiled as he died.
But not a drop, I tell you, brothers serving Justice,
not a drop was spilt on his precious white robe.
Not a drop from that old man's ravenous mouth.

The Cross

My hands have seen
as much horror as my eyes.
Forgive me today, my good friend of old dreams,
forgive me for disrupting your grief again.
Even though my hands shake like a dead branch,
I want to testify about what's happening to our
        orphaned race.

It was in a churchyard,
a mother pleading for her only son,
pulling out her hair.
But who was left to listen?
Every soul wounded.
Every mother next to a dead son.
She was sewing a shroud,
and wiping her eyes with it.

And this delirious woman
with no one to talk to
fell on the dusty stones of the church floor:
"I want my son or my death,
my son or my death."
She lit candles, burned incense,

wailed at the deaf dome above.
When she gave up on God,
she went to the Turks
and kissed their swords,
begging for her boy.

A mob gathered in the churchyard,
returning from more killing.
Beneath a tent—widows, corpses, orphans,
and like hyenas,
the mob came to wipe their swords.

"Your son?—No problem. We'll fetch him.
Isn't he tall and bright-eyed?
The one who fought yesterday trying to defend you?
He's in the vestibule praying for you.
Don't worry, it's his turn, he'll be free today."
Then the gendarmes huddled,
and giggling like croaking ravens,
bowed before her.
"Take off that flowery dress, we need it."

In a minute the men came running out of the vestibule
with a blood-soaked dress.
"Isn't this your dress?
Doesn't it smell familiar? What kind of mother are you?
Smell it, go ahead!
Don't be mad; we sacrificed your son on the altar
with white cloths and candles.

Now we'll paint your cross . . .
bring the nails and the hammers
before the dress dries."

Then one of the Turks took the bloody dress
and painted a cross on the chapel wall.
Beneath the tents the widows buried their heads.

In the church that Turk pointed to the cross.
"Kneel down and pray.
We'll do it to you like you did it to Christ.
Hey mother, pray to your son.
Have you no faith in the resurrection?"

The Son

Take heart, and let me tell you about the heroism
of a farmer who hearing of the bloody news
rode back to his village.
Behind him he left the oxen bellowing
in the burning, tilled fields.
Behind him, the new wheat, the coulter, the spade, the plow.
He left the hope of old days, of his native soil.
No more peaceful work songs,
Now he sang songs of resistance.

The evening sun was torrid and black,
Standing at his doorstep, his terror rose like heat from the earth.
For miles—the cinders of farms, strewn corpses.
And in his living room his wife, naked and stabbed,
her black hair matted with blood.
His son stared at his mother's expression.

At the other end of the village, some Turks heard his horse:
"Let's make sure we've burned everything,
every infidel; there are still sounds, still some breathing."

The Armenian farmer and his son
watched the black mob coming

and shot into the crowd,
while mourners and corpses looked on.
But the mob kept pouring in like sand blown from a
  barren place.
Holding the warm corpse of his wife in one arm
and his son by the waist, he staggered to the riverbank.

The titanic dark was less malevolent than the Turks,
and holding his son and dragging his dead wife
he looked like an uprooted oak as he dove into the
  waters of Sihoun.
He set his wife free in the tide,
and the waves rinsed her blood
as she bobbed from stone to stone like a coffin.

All night the corpses of his countrymen floated around him.
His son was like a wet reed in his arm.
By morning the Mediterranean was a flaming sun
on his face,
and on the beach, among the corpses,
the blue, stiff, rinsed body of his wife—
and he was kissing his son like a lunatic.

Their Song

And one of them called out and
gathered the bloodthirsty crowd around him.

"—Look, this is the horror of the caravan of the righteous,
which passes on top of the prosperous and empty town.
The arms of my army burn and their teeth gnash
as if it were a feast day.

I saw corpses in the garrets of slavery,
and these bodies I snatched because they're infidels.
Allah says: turn the valley of the infidels into graves,
butcher the children, fuck all the virgins.

I designed the war of death and life.
In this fog of ashes and spirits . . .
In this air of blood and fists and bones,
and the useless cries for help,
in the air like stars I sprayed cut heads,
I spread death like a caravan of clouds.

What are you waiting for? It's all yours.
Strike and eat and dance and get drunk . . .
The days, the gold, the women—the Armenians are ours.

Let the wine and dream, the unrighteous blood flow."

Then, someone else orders his horse:
"—Don't spare a life—
Your shoes are forged by Allah.
Dig your hooves into their slave-hearts.
Let's kill, at last, the Armenian fantasy of freedom.
The foam of your tail shines on the ruin.
My sword reaped the black souls and opened the
        gateways of paradise.
Good stallion. Your white hair is red."

Another one shouts to his men through the bugles,
"—It's either them or us.
This is our last chance for paradise.

Blast your bugles.
Your foreheads burn,
And the valleys of the Taurus still need Armenian
        irrigation . . .

There's no law anymore,
and the king of slaves is brute force.
Drink from my cup the blood of young virgins.

Time runs. Justice changes its course. Drink
from this virgin's skull.
What's gold or silver next to this?"

*   *   *

Let their song shake the dead in the earth. . . .
Only the living are motionless, but men and women
        don't cry,

they are motionless like stones.
Only mercy is pitiless, only thought is doubt,
and faith, folly.

The Blind

Making his way with a walking stick,
in a white robe, he moved like death
through the bloodthirsty mob,

"I'm not a stranger, I'm a believer like you.
I'm eighty and I've had no horizon but darkness....
Even if I walk the world groping
it's no different from where I stand:
All pleasure is for you,
you can convict and punish,
skin your victim with your hands,
whatever the law commands in these days of
        righteousness.
I don't even know the visage of the infidel.
What monster, what reptile, what black snake does it
        resemble?
How badly I want to feel a dead body with my hands.
I smell the ashes—
May you live a thousand years, blessed ones—

While walking, my slippers suddenly stick to the earth....
I know what it is ...I smell it.
The blood of sinners is so hot

it's like fire flowing over the roads....

—I've been told that you've already burnt their houses,
the last field, the last stable, huts, and villages and
        towns.
With my petrified eyes, how can I enjoy all this?
Only my ear is happy. Praise Allah!

For the past eight days I hear the cries from
        blasphemous mouths.
Only my ear is happy, the rest illusion...
I'd love to have a sword and swing it
against children, naked women, against geriatrics like me.
I want to mow them all down like reeds.
All the fun is yours. I'm swimming in darkness.
I can't watch for a second.

Where are the piles of corpses?
If my son were here, he'd have pity on me.
The other day I armed him,
anointed him with my blessing and sent him to fight for
        Allah.
Isn't there any among you, a friend, a neighbor,
who would put a dagger in my hand, and bring me a
        fair-haired Armenian girl?

My blindness shouldn't deprive me of my heaven.
Bring me a virgin whose body's tender as a dove.
My hands are unaccustomed ... "

After a while a youth appeared holding an Armenian
  virgin by the hair.
With reverence he said to the blind man:
"Your son is my friend and my father's an old
  acquaintance of yours,

Can you guess who I am?
I've read to you now and then from the Koran.
I chose this girl from the nearby village,
but she wouldn't become a Muslim, and refuses to be
  my wife.
I'm terrified by her eyes, I'm afraid she'll strangle me in
  my bed.

A thousand pities that you're blind, but feel her body first,
imagine this youthful body, hot like a foal.
She's naked; come here to the meadow.
Kneel down, cross your legs, take my dagger.
I know you're not experienced at this—
not that way—fold your thumb over the handle.
Now, give it all you've got, one blow should do it ... "

The naked girl writhed like an enraged wave,
and the red hands that held her, nailed her white rage to
    the meadow,
and she looked like an orphan swan.

Another hand covered her blue eyes with her veil,
and smothered her voice.
Rolling up his sleeves the blind man said in a hoarse way:

"A thousand cheers, I'm ready.
Where is her heart, my son?"

"Wait, let me guide your hand."

As the blood splattered his face
like flaming poppies,
he shouted to the crowd:
"My eyes are clear. I've seen the light."

The Mulberry Tree

I wondered why we were walking with a few
packages of rags in our hands.
The two of us, drifting from one dead village to another.
Then we met an old humped woman,
who approached us with a bag of bread and a walking stick.

"Since morning I've been searching
for the ashes of my house.
Eight days ago Turkish neighbors ruined our village.
My eldest son died in a fight, I'm told.
I performed his last bath in a stream.
Our old neighbors (now our enemies)
took pity on me because of my age,
and like friends—because there were no friends—
they came and buried him a day later
in the orange grove.

Now my eyes are dry and I can't even
cry for my dead grandson.
For eight days I've gone from tent to tent.
No sleep; no waking hours; only dreams.

Let them ruin my world, but spare my grandson. . . .

I screamed 'kill me in my grandson's place, kill me,'
but no one heard.
No one heard and they threw the half-dead boy in the cart
of corpses that passed from the convent.
I still see his eyes. For a long time
they were open—staring at me—as he gave up the ghost.
I still hear the cart creaking."

She sobbed and went on.
"No home. No family. I'm alone with my own death.
You should've seen my home, what a hearth of good
        things—
lambs, hens, a white cock.
Everything in my sheepfold burnt down.
In my granary I had a handful of wheat for autumn,
under my garret two bee-hives.
In one day the whole village was burned.
Every morning smoke puffed out my chimney.
What did the Turks want from me? Tell me. . .
Look over there—the remains of my cottage.
Look at the spring spilling into the brook
under the ruined wall. It waters my ashes.
But what does any of this mean without my grandson?
Give me two stones so that I can crack my head open.
They've even cut down my mulberry tree.
Give me death. They've cut my mulberry tree.
I planted it the day my grandson was born.
They've cut my mulberry tree.
Woe to his memory. It grew tall before my eyes just like
        him—
It was seven years old, and I was sitting in its shade

with my grandson in my arms singing.
They've even cut my mulberry tree.
Look, they sawed it at the roots.
Where is the cart with the corpses? I still hear it squeak.
I want to be thrown into it next to my grandson.
There's still a place on the cart."

It was a horrible sight.
The miserable woman clinging to a sawed-off branch
of a mulberry tree, falling down.
I couldn't hold back my sobs.
And on that road to hell
the young woman I was traveling with
began to cry like a child.

Strangled

And in a dug-out cellar, forty people—
like terrified cattle.

We massed together,
shivering, bruising each other,
and our silence grew into panic
as if we were looking at the Demon.

From sunrise to sunrise,
we were like gravestones, and hungry.
We tried to kill our rage and homesickness,
and the silence was endless space filling our eyes.

Out there, the Turks like thousands of jackals,
not tired from wasting our orchards and villages,
trying to find us.
In the darkness we heard
the flash-dance crackling, flaring in the sun—
guns, spears, bayonets, and swords.
Corpses like uprooted trees
fell on the roof of our cellar.
Through the walls we heard shrieks, mute breathing,
the ghost given up.

Blood seeped through the earth ceiling
and trickled our faces.

Then, a newborn began to squeal.
The mother was sobbing . . .
"God have mercy, my breasts are dry
and he's already sucked my blood."

"We gotta strangle him," someone said.

"It's the only way," the others said.

"Strangle me first, then my son."

"They've heard us, and they're digging, the bastards."

"The child's betrayed us."

"The roof's falling in."

"Christ, a shaft of light."

"I beg you. . . here's my throat."

In the dark, the mother
offered her throat, then her son's . . .

Then like snakes, two arms found the infant,
and the silence in the cellar was a storm.
I thought we had all died.

Then we heard the men above cursing
and the killers left.
Was this salvation? Can slaves be saved?

Every day that mother, half-naked, stands by the road
delirious, hanging on the skirt of the stranger, the
      enemy, the passerby.

"I strangled my baby. It's true.
Have pity on me; I'm a coward.
You could wring my neck in a second.

Have you no heart?"

A Victory

We're opening the town today,
the bulwarks and barricades.
The grieving, the widows, the orphans
depend on us. . . .
We'll walk from village to village, ruin to ruin.
With our brotherly hands we'll gather the helpless,
call them to self-defense, arm them with faith.

To love life is the only way to win.
All who don't have a tawny piece of iron and angry arms,
let them come forward.
In Chok-Marzevan there are plenty of guns and brave men.

The survivors arrive . . .
like a caravan of pain,
bodies without arms, torsos crawling,
old men and women with shattered jaws,
from a hundred abandoned villages . . .
brides and virgins raped, children axed to death in their
                    mothers' laps.
Take anything: flints or spades,
the scythe, a pickaxe, the plough's iron handle.

Let's not have any weeping, either.
Let the hopeless shut up.

We've begged too long in silence.
Enough of frankincense, of the crosses, the sneering God.
Enough of cannibal humanity.
We've been beggars too long, digging out our eyes.
What we've witnessed, centuries haven't witnessed.

For the past seven days Chok-Marzevan
has been parched by a black thirst.
Fountains of Armenian blood in the orange groves.
For seven days we sucked the leaves of the trees
till our tongues were red.
We ate ashes.

For seven dawns and sunsets we
pushed the Turks back.
Our call for brotherhood was unheard,
and our soldier bearing the message of peace
came back wrapped in a white flag.

What makes the Turks tick?
They have no Ideals, frankly, they have no ideas.
They spew the pestilence of their religion,
for the quick pleasures of plunder.

Our women have turned all the copper and lead, the tin
            and brass into bullets and bayonets.
Our moments are centuries. Keep firing.
Our conscience is calm.

Our fatherland is rubble.
The Turks are not real citizens,
but worms in the mud pile of brotherhood
we dreamt of for so long.

Knock off that guy in the turban and the one with a flag
reading his sermons to madden the crowd.
Keep firing so the foreign warships sleeping in the
           Dardanelles can hear us.

My chest is cut open,
but . . . use my body as a barricade.

Victory, brothers.
The starry sky in your irises.
Fire!

Select Bibliography on Siamantʿō
(Adom Yarjanian)

Works by Siamantʿō

Tiwts ʿaznōrē ʿn [Heroically], Paris, 1902.

Hayortinerĕ [The Sons of Armenia], Geneva: Trōshag, 1905.

Hayortinerĕ [The Sons of Armenia], Second Series, Geneva: Trōshag, 1906.

Hayortinerĕ [The Sons of Armenia], Third Series, Paris: Hamazkayin Dbaran, 1908.

Hokevark ʿi ew boysi chaber [Torches of Despair and Hope], Rʿupen Zartarean, intro., Paris: Hamazkayin Dbaran, 1907.

Garmir lurer paregamēʾs [Bloody News from My Friend], *Aztag* Literature Series no. 1, Constantinople: "Ardziw" Zhoghovrtagan Kravajar ʿanotsʿ, 1909.

Ampoghchagan kordzĕ [Complete Works], vol. 1, Boston: Dbaran Hayrenikʿ, 1910 [incomplete; includes only: *Heroically, Torches of Despair and Hope, The Call to the Homeland*, and *Bloody News from My Friend*].

Surp Mesrob [St. Mesrob], Constantinople; ŏ. Arzuman, 1913.

Ĕndir erger [Selected Works], Soghomon Darontsʿi, ed., Serop Sarksyan, comp., introd. by Eghishē Bedrosyan, Yerevan: Haybedhrad, 1957.

Ampoghchagan kordz [Complete Works], Cairo, 1960.

Works about Siamantʿō

Hrand Tʿamrazean, *Siamantʿō*, Yerevan: Haybedhrad, 1964.

Hegdor Rʿshduni, *Siamantʿō*, Yerevan: Hayasdan, 1970.

K. Kh. Sdepʿanyan, ed., K. H. Aznavuryan, compiler and annotator, *Arevmdahay kroghneri namagani: Kragan zharʿankut ʿyun* [Correspondence of Western Armenian Writers: Literary Legacy], Book VI, Part 1, Yerevan: Erevani Bedagan Hamalsaran, Eghishe Chʿarentsʿi anvan Kraganutʿyan ev arvesdi tʿankaran, 1972.

Select Bibliography

Yeghishē Bedrosyan, *Kragan Temk`er* [Literary Figures], Yerevan; Sovedagan Krogh, 1977, pp. 3-114.

Serkey Sarinyan, "Adom Yarjanyan-Siamant`ō," chapter 5 in Sarinyan et al., *Hay nor kraganut`yan padmut`yun* [History of Modern Armenian Literature], Yerevan: Haygagan SSH Kidut`yunneri Agàdemia, M. Apeghyani anvan Kraganut`yan Insdidud, 1979, pp. 471-501.

H[agop]. Ōshagan, *Hamabadger arewmdahay kraganut`ean, ut`erort hador: Aruesdake`d Serunt* [Panorama of Western Armenian Literature, Eighth Volume: The Artistic Generation], Ant`ilias, Lebanon; Gat`oghigosut`iwn Hayots` Medzi Dann Giligioy, 1980, pp. 215-77.